My World of ANIMALS™

CATS

FRANCES E. RUFFIN

The Rosen Publishing Group's
PowerKids Press™
New York

For Elizabeth Marie Ruffin

Published in 2004 by The Rosen Publishing Group, Inc.
29 East 21st Street, New York, NY 10010

Copyright © 2004 by The Rosen Publishing Group, Inc.

First Edition

Book Design: Mike Donnellan
Illustration by Mike Donnellan

Photo Credits: Cover © Digital Vision; pp. 5, 7, 9, 11, 13, 17, 19, 21 © Royalty-Free/CORBIS; p. 15 © Orion/International Stock.

Ruffin, Frances E.
Cats / Frances E. Ruffin.
p. cm. — (My world of animals)
Includes bibliographical references and index.
Summary: This book introduces cats, describing their habitats and behavior.
ISBN 1-4042-2521-8 (lib.)
1. Cats—Juvenile literature   [1. Cats]   I. Title   II. Series
SF445.7.R835 2004   2003-010261
636.8—dc21

Manufactured in the United States of America

CONTENTS

Cats live in homes around the world.

Cats lick their fur to
keep it clean.

Claws help cats to climb trees.

When a cat is scared, it raises its back. Its fur stands up.

A cat's eyes become round and large in the dark. This helps it to see well when there is very little light.

A cat lands on its feet when it falls. Cats can be hurt if they fall from a very high place.

A cat purrs for many reasons. It may purr when you hold it, or when it wants to eat.

Holding and petting a cat can make a person feel good.

Cats and dogs can be best friends.

WORDS TO KNOW

back

claws

eyes

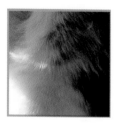

fur

Here are more books to read about cats:

All About Cats and Kittens
by Emily Neye
All Aboard Books

Know Your Cat
by Bruce Fogle
DK Publishing

Due to the changing nature of Internet links, PowerKids Press has developed an online list of Web sites related to the subject of this book. This site is updated regularly. Please use this link to access the list:

www.powerkidslinks.com/mwanim/cat/

INDEX

Word Count: 114

Note to Parents, Teachers, and Librarians

PowerKids Readers are specially designed to help emergent and beginning readers build their skills in reading for information. Simple vocabulary and concepts are paired with real-life photographs or stunning, detailed images from the natural world. Readers will respond to written language by linking meaning with their own everyday experiences and observations. Sentences are short and simple, employing a basic vocabulary of sight words, as well as new words that describe objects or processes that take place in the natural world. Large type, clean design, and photographs corresponding directly to the text all help children to decipher meaning. Features such as a contents page, picture glossary, and index help children to get the most out of PowerKids Readers. They also introduce children to the basic elements of a book, which they will encounter in their future reading experiences. Lists of related books and Web sites encourage kids to explore other sources and to continue the process of learning.